PANDORA

PANDORA

STORY AND PICTURES BY

Clare Turlay Newberry

FELIS BOOKS
SANTA FE • NEW MEXICO

To
The American Society for the Humane Treatment of Animals
The Animal Legal Defense Fund
The Humane Society of the United States
and to all the dedicated, unfunded, volunteer local groups
who rescue, foster and adopt
our furry friends,
including many of the cats and dogs featured in my mother's books.

ONE morning Peter stood in the kitchenette, watching his mother get breakfast. The cereal was bubbling noisily on the stove—GLUP GLUP-GLUP GLUP it went—the coffee was perking in the percolator, and the egg beater whirred loudly as his mother beat eggs in a yellow bowl.

Peter, who was four, was just tall enough to see on top of the kitchen table. He stood very close to his mother so as not to miss anything. Every time she wanted a cup or a spoon she had to reach over and around his little blond head. And every time she took a step she had to look down to see that she didn't walk on Pandora the cat, who sat on the floor at her feet, staring up at her with large anxious green eyes.

"Me-ow!" remarked Pandora plaintively. She rose up on her hind legs and put her forepaws on the edge of the table. "Me-OW!" she repeated.

"Oh, pussy, get down!" exclaimed his mother impatiently. "You're such a nuisance!"

"What does Pandora say, Mummy?" demanded Peter.

"Nothing, Peter, nothing. She just says me-ow," replied his mother shortly. She was squeezing the orange juice and toasting the toast and stirring the cereal and scrambling the eggs and keeping an eye on the

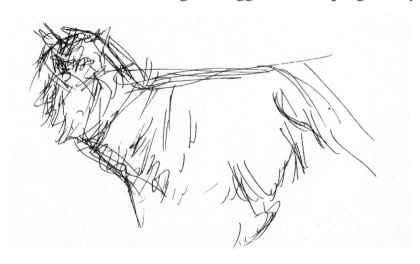

coffee, and she did not feel like conversation. Peter, however, was not discouraged.

"Tell me, Mummy. Tell me!" he insisted, "What does she REALLY say?"

"She says she's hungry," answered his mother. "Darling, why don't you go in the other room and talk to Daddy for awhile? Or play some nice music on the radio?"

Peter did not budge.

"If she's hungry then why doesn't she drink her milk?" he asked, for Pandora had been served her breakfast before anyone else. There it stood under the sink, a nice bowl of warm milk, and she scorned it utterly.

"She wants meat," said his mother, "but there isn't any in the house, so she will just have to wait till we go to the store.... Oh, no, you don't, pussy!" She grabbed Pandora just as she was scrambling into the ice box, hauled her out by the hind legs, and slammed the door.

"Why can't you be a good cat, and behave yourself?"

"There isn't any meat in there, pussy," said Peter tenderly. "You will just have to wait till we go to the store. She will just have to wait, won't she, Mummy?"

"Indeed she will. Come, darling, sit down now and eat your breakfast," said his mother. She set a bowl of cereal on the table in the breakfast nook, tied his napkin on him, and went back to the kitchenette.

When she returned a minute later with the coffee, she found Pandora on the table, greedily lapping Peter's milk. Peter looked on in delight.

"Pandora! You awful cat!"

"Oh, Mummy, please let her stay!" begged Peter. He would have liked nothing better than to share all his meals with Pandora. His mother, however, was grown-up and felt differently.

"Certainly not!" she cried indignantly, hastily removing Pandora. And his father, coming into the room, added firmly, "No animals allowed on the table at mealtime. Better put her in the bathroom, dear, so we can eat in peace."

So Pandora was carried out and shut up in the bathroom.

When breakfast was over Peter's father kissed them good-bye and left for the office.

"Now can Pandora come out, Mummy?" asked Peter.

"Of course, dear," replied his mother, a little sorry that she had been cross with her. "Poor kitty, I forgot all about her, she's been so quiet. I guess she was taking a catnap, curled up in the washbowl." Smiling fondly at the thought she opened the bathroom door.

She gave a little shriek.

"Pandora! Oh, you awful, AWFUL cat!"

Pandora, perched high on a shelf, was daintily pulling the tissues out of a box of Kleenex. Reaching a long arm into the box she would slowly draw out a sheet, tear it into bits, and watch them flutter to the floor. The room was littered with shredded Kleenex. When she heard Peter's mother she dropped hastily to the floor, scampered into the living room, and disappeared under the sofa.

A moment later she crept cautiously out, her eyes gleaming with mischief. Suddenly she caught sight of Peter. Up went her back like a Halloween cat, her fur stood on end, and she pranced sideways on her tiptoes, glaring and spitting. This was the beginning of her favorite game, in which she pretended that Peter was a Dangerous Enemy.

"Ow-w—wah-wah-wah—WOW!" she wailed, shrinking back as though terrified. Then she sprang at him.

"MUMMY! MUMMY!" he shrieked and clattered down the hall with the cat at his heels. At the end of the hall they stopped and faced each other, staring fixedly into each other's eyes. Pandora held his gaze as long as she could, then with a muffled howl she turned and skittered madly back into the living room.

Whooping joyfully Peter dashed after her. Again she vanished under the sofa, crept out and charged at him as before, and again he tore down the hall, screaming as if wolves were after him. Up and down the length of the apartment they raced, taking turns chasing each other and making a most dreadful racket.

Today the game wound up in the living room. It was hard to say now who was chasing whom as the child and cat frisked about, making sudden dashes at each other and then running in circles. Peter made the most noise, but Pandora ran the fastest. Around and around the room she flew, taking long leaps from one piece of furniture to another. She scarcely touched the floor.

At last she sailed to the top of a door, and clung there by her front paws, kicking wildly.

"Look out, Pandora! You'll fall down!" yelled Peter, dancing with excitement. But Pandora did not fall. She managed to scramble to the top of the door, where she wobbled back and forth for a moment like a tightrope walker at the circus. Then she took off for the nearest bookcase. As she landed she collided with a tall vase, which fell to the floor with a CRASH!

"What on earth—" cried Peter's mother, running into the room. Then she saw the broken vase.

"My lovely vase! Oh, Peter, how did it happen?"

"BOOM!" shouted Peter. "Pandora bumped into it and it went BOOM and broke all—to—pieces!"

"Pandora is the worst cat I ever knew!" cried his mother as she knelt down to pick up the pieces of the broken vase.

Peter looked grieved.

"But, Mummy," he said reproachfully, "she didn't mean to do it. She skidded."

He put his arms around Pandora, who purred violently and gave him a quick cat-kiss on the nose.

"She's a perfect nuisance just the same," said his mother. "Oh well, it can't be helped now." She put the larger pieces of the vase in the wastebasket, and got the broom and dustpan to sweep up the rest.

"Don't you think you might play quietly for awhile, darling?" she asked. "Why don't you go in your room and color some pictures in your drawing book while Mummy cleans up in here? Go on, that's a good boy."

Peter was about to protest, but something told him that his mother was in no mood for an argument. "All right, Mummy," he said affably, and galloped off to his room with Pandora at his heels.

Peter got the crayons out of the top drawer of his bureau, and lying down on his stomach began to color one of the pages in his drawing book, an outline picture of a Shetland pony and some very old-fashioned children. He colored the pony purple and the children yellow and green, adding pink squiggles around the margin to make it look pretty.

Pandora wanted to pat the crayons but he shooed her away. "Don't bother me now, kitty," he said, frowning impatiently, "can't you see I'm busy?" So presently she gave up and sauntered off by herself.

After a bit Peter's mother came into the room. "Put your things away now, darling," she said briskly, "we're going to the store." She helped him pick up the crayons and put them back in the bureau drawer. Then they went out to do the marketing.

When they returned, laden with groceries, Pandora did not come to meet them as she usually did. Even when Peter's mother put some meat on the floor and called, "Kitty, kitty, kitty!" she did not appear.

"That's odd," said his mother, "I wonder where she can be."

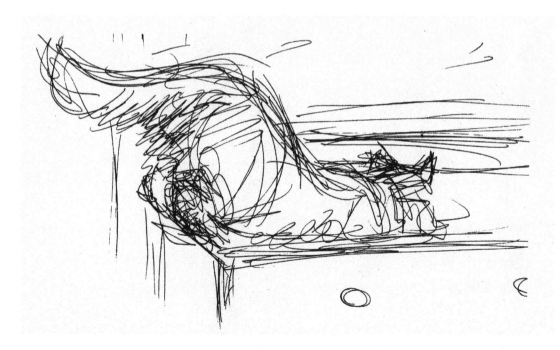

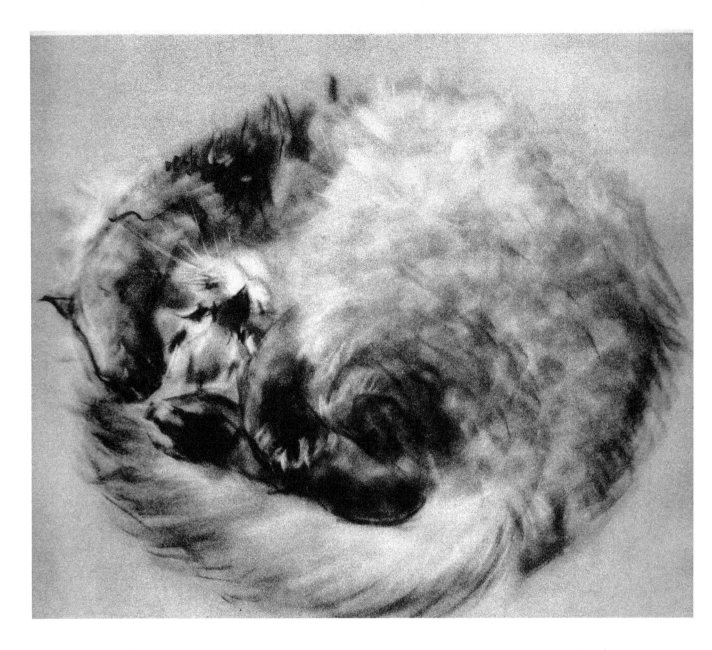

She went quickly through the apartment, glancing under the beds and sofa, and throwing open the clothes closets and broom cupboard, where Pandora sometimes got shut up by mistake. But there were no signs of her.

"Where is she, Mummy? Where is she? Tell me!" asked Peter.

"Oh, she's around here somewhere," his mother assured him. "She can't have got out."

They searched the apartment again, more carefully this time, peering into the linen closet and the clothes hamper and the icebox and the gas oven. They looked in the Victrola and the writing desk, and Peter's mother stood on a chair and explored the top shelves of the clothes closets. She got down on her hands and knees and rummaged around in the dark corners among the sandals and galoshes and old shoes. But still they didn't find Pandora.

"She can't have got out," his mother repeated, but she wasn't so sure of it now. Distressing pictures flashed across her mind—Pandora, so fluffy and innocent, flitting down the stairs and out into the street, to be swallowed up forever in the stream of city traffic. Pandora, thin and bedraggled, mewing weakly at passers-by for food. At this point

Peter's mother ran to the door of the apartment, flung it open, and stared up and down the empty corridor.

"Did Pandora go away, Mummy?" demanded Peter anxiously. "Did she? TELL me!"

"Peter, I don't know!" exclaimed his mother, almost in tears.

Then they heard her—a faint and far-off mew.

"Mummy!" shouted Peter. "She's here!"

"Be still, Peter," commanded his mother. "Listen."

"Mee—e—e—OW—W—W!" There it was again. It seemed to be closer this time. But where did it come from?

"It sounds as if she were in one of the walls!" cried his mother in bewilderment, and she ran about distractedly, almost tripping over Peter, who darted ahead of her like an eager puppy.

"I've looked every possible place a cat could be!" she declared

wildly, and now she began looking in all the IMPOSSIBLE places—the breadbox and the coffee percolator and the medicine cabinet in the bathroom, places where there simply wasn't room for a full-grown cat.

The mews became louder. Wherever Pandora was, it was plain that she wanted to get out. Finally she was yowling in real earnest, and scratching about frantically in her hiding place. All at once they both knew where she was.

"The bureau!" cried Peter's mother, and they rushed into Peter's room and yanked open the top drawer. Out sprang Pandora, rumpled and indignant.

"Rr—PWRR!" she exclaimed wrathfully. She did not wait to be petted but made a dash for the kitchenette. What SHE wanted was meat.

Peter ran after her and threw himself on the floor to watch her eat.

"What did Pandora say when she was in the drawer?" he wanted to know.

"She said, 'Let me out! Let me out!' " replied his mother, who was starting to prepare lunch.

"And what did she say when we let her out?"

"She said, 'WELL! It's about time!' "

Peter chuckled.

"Why didn't she tell us where she was?"

"Because she's only a kitty, and kitties don't know how to explain things very well," said his mother.

"She's only a kitty, and kitties don't know how to 'splain things," echoed Peter wisely. "What does she say right now?"

"Oh, Peter, she doesn't say anything," his mother answered wearily. "She's eating her lunch."

"Well, then, what does she THINK?"

"Darling, I don't know!"

"Yes, you DO, Mummy! Tell me! TELL me!"

His mother sighed.

"Well...she is thinking how glad she is that she has a good home where everybody loves her.... And she is glad she has plenty to eat.... And that she belongs to a nice little yellow-haired boy named Peter. And that's all. That's absolutely ALL!" said Peter's mother.

About the artist's process creating *PANDORA*

After her hit books, *HERBERT THE LION, MITTENS, BABETTE,* and receiving Caldecott Honors for *BARKIS, APRIL'S KITTENS* and *MARSHMALLOW,* Clare Turlay Newberry was lauded by the *New York Times* for creating "the very best cat pictures that have ever been made."

Still working to raise her artwork to ever higher levels, in 1943 Clare discovered a book by an art teacher who changed her experience of art for the rest of her life. He was Kimon Nicolaides, possibly the most brilliant art teacher in the history of American art. Nicolaides had taught at the Art Students League in New York, training many who would become leading artists. After his death in 1938, his students had compiled his methods to finish his revolutionary book, *THE NATURAL WAY TO DRAW*. This book outlined a year of study in a variety of techniques and media. Clare committed herself to it completely.

Nicolaides began teaching new students with this statement, "The sooner you make your first five thousand mistakes the sooner you will be able to correct them." The drawing exercises included drawing without looking at the paper, drawing in wild scribbles to capture the essence of a movement or a form, rather than the usual careful duplication of a figure. As Nicolaides often said, "You should draw not what the thing looks like, not even what it is, but what it is doing.... Gesture has no precise edges, no forms. The forms are in the act of changing. Gesture is movement in space."

It took courage to follow Nicolaides process, and to complete this year of training outlined in *THE NATURAL WAY TO DRAW* required Clare to draw hundreds of drawings a day and then to simply toss them into the rubbish as unimportant. These exercises finely tuned her hand-eye coordination so perfectly that for Clare to see a cat was enough for her hand to draw it. Clare was completely absorbed and had found her way, at last, to become the best artist she could be.

This rather Zen-like approach demanded that Clare approach drawing as if she, called "the best cat artist since the Egyptians" by *TIME* Magazine, knew nothing and had to start from scratch. The Nicolaides process worked, and Clare's work evolved again, this time to a three-dimensional level that has never been equaled and is still prized by child fans, former child fans, and artists alike.

PANDORA, Clare's very next book, showed the quantum leap her work had taken after studying Nicolaides. Published in 1944, *PANDORA* was done in yet another new medium Clare developed to make cats come so alive on paper that they seemed ready to walk off the page. She perfected using pastels on velour paper, and chose a long-haired Persian kitty, Pandora, as her heroine. In a daring move, she also included wild, free ink sketches usually only shared between artists, and never presented to the public.

PANDORA was a hit, and not just with owners of Persian kitties, either. Artists, cat fanciers, and children all loved the rich, three-dimensional, velvety drawings of Pandora portrayed with the personality of a real feline—both maddening and delightful. Also, due to Clare's popularity, this was the first book her publishers had allowed her to do in color to capture her velvety greys, an expensive process in those days.

Excerpts from *THE CAT ARTIST: The Story of Clare Turlay Newberry*, written by her daughter, Felicia N. Trujillo, with covers and illustrations from all of her mother's works printed in full color.

CHAPTER ONE: IN THE VERY
BEGINNING
THERE WERE CATS

Clare's story begins in the tiny town of Enterprise, Oregon, April 10, 1903. Clare Wasson Turlay was born just twenty-five miles from the homestead log cabin in which her mother, Daisy Wasson, had spent her childhood. Clare often told me the story of how Daisy's pioneer parents, Joseph Thompson Wasson and Jennie Blevans Wasson, had settled on a long green ridge called the Cat's Back, eighteen miles from the nearest cabin east of the town of Joseph, Oregon. A young homesteading couple very much in love, Daisy's parents built a small cabin surrounded by an awesome amphitheater carved between the Seven Devils Mountains and the Eagle Mountains with their clear creeks and deep canyons.

Clare, however, was born in her Aunt Allie Hyatt's hobbit-like miniature Victorian in Enterprise, which had been built for her by her husband, George Hyatt, and has remained a town favorite. When I visited the Hyatt House, I could barely fit my size-eight shoes on the diminutive steps and wondered how Clare's mother, Daisy, had somehow wedged herself up the narrow staircase to where Clare was born in the bedroom at the top. A single stained glass window lit the dark wooden stairs as I climbed back through time.

Dark-eyed Daisy, Clare's mother, on left, and her Aunt Caroline, on right, with their beloved pets and family guitar. September 5, 1900

The Hyatt House in Enterprise, Oregon

Once we were old enough to read, all the children in our family grew up reading Grandma Daisy's manuscript, *Around the Cat's Back,* for decades before the Oregon Historical Society published it in 1989. Drawn from Daisy's childhood diary, these touching stories about her pioneer family homesteading in northeast Oregon depict a love of the family animals that presaged Clare's unusual empathy with cats and dogs.

Although Daisy's pioneer family may have lacked drawing materials and had to create their own entertainment playing guitar and singing old family songs, they were never deprived of cats and a number of other animals that were considered family, including their pet hens, dogs and horses. This heartfelt appreciation of animals is shown by the fact that some of Clare's very first drawings were of the Turlay family cats.

The family sense of whimsy was revealed in the novel names the Wassons invented for their pets. Their dogs had commoner names like Rover and Minnie and their horses were called Topsy, Coalie, Old Nell, Flax and Jude. More innovative names were awarded to Daisy's beloved pet hen, Hecate, and a multitude of cats named Polly, Stranger, Leslie, Rindy, Randy, Shiny Top, Noah, Midget I and II, Smut, Dick Marmaduke, Play the Fiddle Play the Fiddle, Tom Tittlemouse, Croppie (whose ear tips had been cut off), Robert E. Lee and Tab Greengage Simply Him Play the Drum Play the Drum.

Clare's parents' wedding portrait

DRAWING AT TWO. As Clare told interviewers,

> *"According to my mother, I began drawing just before my second birthday, and from then on pencils, crayons, and later watercolors were favorite playthings. I always adored kittens and drew them from the very beginning. At six or seven I began to want to be an illustrator of fairy tales and in my teens I spent a good deal of time making careful watercolor pictures for my favorite stories."*

GROWING UP VICTORIAN. It is odd for me to realize that Clare grew up in the Victorian era of Sherlock Holmes, with furniture that resembled teddy bears—all round, velvety and solid. There was also the rich plethora of stained-glass lamps, with fringes and beads, and plush carpets and things made well and made of heavy materials; things made to work and to last forever.

Clare, age ten, 1913

Clare was named after her father, Chester Clare Turlay, who was half American Indian and half British. Despite prejudice against him for being a "half-breed," Chester rode on horseback across Oregon and Washington states putting up the first electrical wires and was a self-made millionaire by age 25. He courted and wed Daisy Wasson, "the prettiest girl" in Wallowa County, Oregon.

Clare's mother, Daisy.

In 1921, at age eighteen, Clare attended a year at the University of Oregon, followed by another year at the School of the Portland Art Museum, and then traveled to the big city of San Francisco to attend the California School of Fine Arts, later known as the San Francisco Art Institute. Then at age 26, Clare went to Paris and began her studies at the Académie de la Grande Chaumière with the intention of becoming a children's portrait painter, but it was there that she began work on the illustrations for what would become her first best seller.

HERBERT THE LION was so popular that it remained in print for decades and then was reissued again in 1998 by a brilliant young editor, Elizabeth Sullivan, as part of Smithmark Publishers' "Clare Newberry Classics." Known for their painstaking reproduction of classics, Smithmark began to republish Clare's books just as they looked when generations of children first fell in love with them.

For more information on all of Clare Turlay Newberry's books, background photographs and stories, and her daughter's biography, *THE CAT ARTIST*, see *www.NewberryCats.com*

For more insider stories and pics, see the Clare Turlay Newberry Group Facebook page and join if you wish!

ACKNOWLEDGMENTS

I am most grateful to my brother, Stephen Newberry, and his wife, Jinny,
my literary agent, Irene Kraas,
Suzan Hall, Bari Dubois of CatHappy.net,
my mother, Clare Newberry Trujíllo, and my father, Henry V. Trujíllo,
without whose help publishing these books would not have happened.

ABOUT FELICIA N. TRUJÍLLO

When Felicia was seven years old her mother, Clare Newberry Trujíllo, began teaching her to draw from life, write and lay out books. This early training prepared Felicia to head the Medical Graphics Department at San Francisco General Hospital/UC Medical Center and other Bay Area hospitals, where she created public health education materials until she began her training as a Patient Advocate and fell in love with pre-med studies. She studied with Dr. Moshé Feldenkrais, D.Sc., graduating in 1983, and has taught his applications of neuroscience ever since. Felicia lives in Santa Fe, New Mexico, with the most feline of canines, her small rescued Schnauzer.